love purposefully. give generously. live expectantly.

DON HAMILTON

FOREWORD BY GREG NETTLE

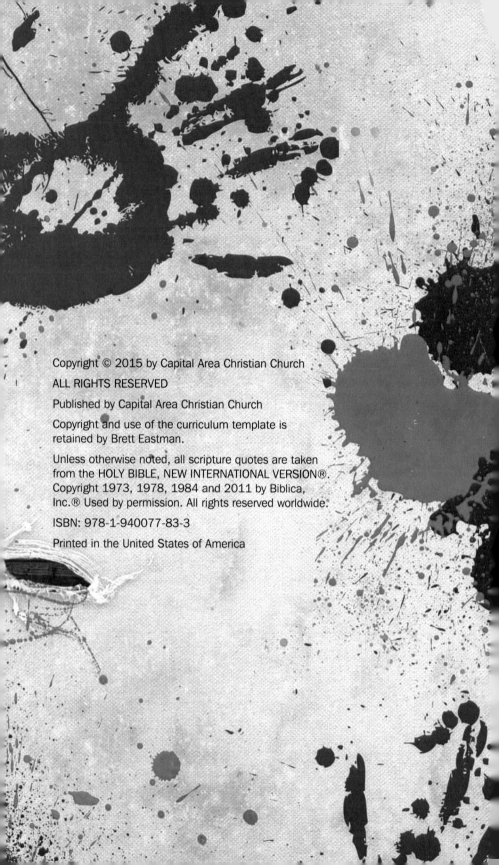

CONTENTS

Foreword by

GREG NETTLE

I walked into my home office and found an envelope lying on the keyboard of my laptop computer. On the front of the envelope it simply said, "For God's churches."

Just a few weeks prior, after serving as Senior Pastor of RiverTree Christian Church for twenty-five years, I announced that I would be transitioning into a new role as President of Stadia global church planting. Stadia plants churches that intentionally care for children. With new church planting remaining the single most effective way of reaching people who are far away from Jesus, and with 85% of those who make a decision to follow Jesus doing so between the ages of four and fourteen—transitioning to Stadia was a crystal clear call of God on my life.

Over the years, RiverTree had become a very generous church. A church that cares for children. A church that cares deeply for those who are far away from God. A church a whole lot like CACC.

As I transitioned from RiverTree to Stadia, the Elders of RiverTree wanted to honor my 25 years of service with a departing gift. A new truck? Family vacation? Golf clubs? Believe me, all of these things were very enticing. In the end, I did ask for a gift. I asked for RiverTree to plant a church in Colombia in partnership with Stadia and Compassion International. A church that would reach people who are far away from Jesus. A church that would intentionally care for children. Why? Because that's what love does.

But this is not my story. Not really. It's actually my daughter Tabitha's story. Fifteen-year-old Tabitha is the one who put the envelope on my computer keyboard. Tabitha is the one who wrote the words, "For God's churches," o the front of the envelope. Tabitha is the one who filled the envelope with every dollar she had saved: $196. Why would a freshman in high school give every cent she had to plant new churches in Colombia? Because that's what love does.

As I sat at my desk and my eyes filled with tears in response to my daughter's generosity, several thoughts ran through my mind. "Oh Tabitha, I am so proud of you. Tabitha, you have invested in something that is so close to your father's heart. Tabitha, because you have been faithful, I as your father, cannot wait to entrust you with more. Because of your generosity I will do everything I possibly can to give you every good thing that you desire." Why? Because that's what love does.

And because God is love . . . that's what God does.

God is looking for individuals, churches, organizations, families and businesses to whom He can entrust His resources. He is looking for you. And He is watching to see what you will do with what He has entrusted to you. And when you are generous He will entrust you with more. When you give to others, He is anxious to give back to you. When you invest in things that are close to your Father's heart, He smiles down upon you and absolutely cannot wait to give you every good thing. Why? Because that's what love does.

In the end, RiverTree gave $160,000 as my farewell gift. Enough to plant two new churches that now care for more than 400 children in South America. And I am so thankful. But the gift that matters most to me is the one that God placed in my own home; Tabitha. The gift that Tabitha gave. The gift that revealed Tabitha's heart. The gift that made me, as her father, want to give her so much more. That's the gift that matters most to me. Why? Because that's what love does.

I am so excited that CACC is embarking on this journey of Love Does. I cannot wait to see what God does in and through you as a church. I am looking forward to the stories of generosity that will reveal your heart to the heart of your Father.

I am praying for you and with you. I am walking beside you. I am cheering you on!

Why?

Because that's what love does.

Introduction by
DON HAMILTON

I sat in the meeting when the discussion began and I suddenly sensed déjà vu. As participants began expressing their opinions and frustrations about some dysfunction of the organization, I realized that I had heard it all before, more than once! The meeting progressed and I became more frustrated. "Why are we talking about this again?" I thought. "I thought they were going to do something about this when we discussed it at last years' meeting."

I'll bet you've been there, done that, too? Two of my favorite sayings go like this. "Talk is cheap," and, "When all is said and done, there's usually a lot more said than done." Politicians are famous for this malady, but even in Bible times the same problem existed. The Apostle Paul encountered this attitude in Athens. "It should be explained that all the Athenians as well as the foreigners in Athens seemed to spend all their time discussing the latest ideas." (Acts 17:21 NLT) Too much talk and not enough action.

LOVE DOES

It is comforting to know that God does not operate this way. One simple, famous sentence from the Bible explains how God handles things. "For God so loved the world that He gave . . ." (John 3:16a NLT) God's good intentions and strong words have always been backed by decisive action. He doesn't just talk about love; He does something about; He doesn't just review the problem of sin in the world over and over, He does something about it. In short, we might say with God, love does.

God is kind, love does. God is merciful, love does. God is full of grace and truth, love does. God is a forgiver, love does. God is compassionate, love does. God is generous, love does. When God feels something or sees a problem, He doesn't just talk about it, He does something about it.

This attribute of God is seen nowhere better than through His generosity. He loves to give in every way. Paul put it this way in Titus 3:4-7 (NLT) *"But—When God our Savior revealed his kindness and love, he saved us, not because of the righteous things we had done, but because of his mercy. He washed away our sins, giving us a new birth and new life through the Holy Spirit. He generously poured out the Spirit upon us through Jesus Christ our Savior. Because of his grace he declared us righteous and gave us confidence that we will inherit eternal life."* He "saved us," "washed away our sins," "gave us new birth," "new life," "the Holy Spirit," "Jesus Christ," "declared us righteous," "gave us eternal life!" God is indeed a generous Father! With God, love does.

For the next five weeks, let's take a journey together, learning about the generosity of God and how we, as His children, can and should be generous with our time, talents, testimony, and treasure. Many of our greatest experiences in life are the result of generosity. Generous people are happy people and they get the opportunity to see the hand of God upon their lives.

So join a Life Group, invite a friend, and prepare to see firsthand how Love Does.

Because Love Does,
Pastor Don

USING THIS WORKBOOK

TOOLS TO HELP YOU HAVE A GREAT
LIFE GROUP EXPERIENCE!

1. Notice in the Contents there are three sections: *Sessions*; *Appendices*; and *Life Group Leaders*. Familiarize yourself with the Appendices. Some of them will be used in the sessions themselves.

2. If you are facilitating/leading or co-leading a small group, the section *Life Group Leaders* will give you some experiences of others that will encourage you and help you avoid many common obstacles to effective small group leadership.

3. Use this workbook as a guide, not a straightjacket. If the group responds to the lesson in an unexpected but honest way, go with that. If you think of a better question than the next one in the lesson, ask it. Take to heart the insights included in the *Frequently Asked Questions* pages and the *Life Group Leaders* section.

4. Enjoy your Life Group experience.

5. Pray before each session—for each of your group members, for your time together, and for wisdom and insights.

6. Read the *Outline for Each Session* on the next pages so that you understand how the sessions will flow.

OUTLINE OF EACH SESSION

A TYPICAL GROUP SESSION FOR THE *LOVE DOES* STUDY WILL INCLUDE THE FOLLOWING SECTIONS. READ THROUGH THIS TO GET A CLEAR IDEA OF HOW EACH GROUP MEETING WILL BE STRUCTURED:

WEEKLY MEMORY VERSES

Each session opens with a Memory Verse that emphasizes an important truth from the session. This is an optional exercise, but we believe that memorizing scripture can be a vital part of filling our minds with God's will for our lives. We encourage you to give this important habit a try. The verses for our five sessions are also listed in the appendix.

INTRODUCTION

Each lesson opens with a brief thought that will help you prepare for the session and get you thinking about the particular subject you will explore with your group. Make it a practice to read these before the session. You may want to have the group read them aloud.

SHARE YOUR STORY

The foundation for spiritual growth is an intimate connection with God and His family. You build that connection by sharing your story with a few people who really know you and who earn your trust. This section includes some simple questions to get you talking—letting you share as much or as little of your story as you feel comfortable doing. Each session typically offers you two options. You can get to know your whole group by using the icebreaker question(s), or you can check in with one or two group members, your spiritual partner(s), for a deeper connection and encouragement in your spiritual journey.

HEAR GOD'S STORY

In this section, you'll read the Bible and listen to teaching, in order to hear God's story—and begin to see how His story aligns with yours. When the study directs you to, you'll pop in the DVD and watch a short teaching segment. You'll then have an opportunity to read a passage of scripture, and discuss both the teaching and the text. You won't focus on accumulating information but on how you should live in light of the Word of God. We want to help you apply the insights from scripture practically and creatively, from your heart as well as your head. At the end of the day, allowing the timeless truths from God's Word to transform our lives in Christ should be your greatest aim.

STUDY NOTES

This brief section provides additional commentary, background or insights on the passage you'll study in the *Hear God's Story* section.

CREATE A NEW STORY

God wants you to be a part of His Kingdom—to weave your story into His. That will mean change. It will require you to go His way rather than your own. This won't happen overnight, but it should happen steadily. By making small, simple choices, we can begin to change our direction. This is where the Bible's instructions to "be doers of the Word, not just hearers" (James 1:22) comes into play. Many people skip

over this aspect of the Christian life because it's scary, relationally awkward, or simply too much work for their busy schedules. But Jesus wanted all of His disciples to know Him personally, carry out His commands, and help outsiders connect with Him. This doesn't necessarily mean preaching on street corners. It could mean welcoming newcomers, hosting a short-term group in your home, or walking through this study with a friend. In this study, you'll have an opportunity to go beyond Bible study to biblical living. This section will also have a question or two that will challenge you to live out your faith by serving others, sharing your faith, and worshiping God.

FOR ADDITIONAL STUDY

If you have time and want to dig deeper into more Bible passages about the topic at hand, we've provided additional passages and questions, which you can use either during the meeting, or as homework. Your group may choose to read and prepare before each meeting in order to cover more biblical material. Or, group members can use the additional study section during the week after the meeting. If you prefer not to do study homework, this section will provide you with plenty to discuss within the group. These options allow individuals or the whole group to expand their study while still accommodating those who can't do homework or are new to your group.

DAILY DEVOTIONS

Each week on the *Daily Devotions* pages, we provide scriptures to read and reflect on between sessions. This provides you with a chance to slow down, read just a small portion of scripture each day, and reflect and pray through it. You'll then have a chance to journal your response to what you've read. Use this section to seek God on your own throughout the week. This time at home should begin and end with prayer. Don't get in a hurry; take enough time to hear God's direction.

LOVE DOES
GENEROUSLY

He saved us through the washing of rebirth and
renewal by the Holy Spirit, whom he poured out on us
generously through Jesus Christ our Savior, so that,
having been justified by his grace, we might become
heirs having the hope of eternal life.
Titus 3:5-7

When a couple has a baby, friends and family watch eagerly to see who it will look like. Often the mom and dad have to listen to every aunt, uncle and grandparent remark that the little child "is the spitting image of grandma" or "looks just like my brother."

In your physical appearance, you may resemble several members of your family. But as Christ followers, we are called to "look like" our Father. As we learn more about His character, as we allow the Holy Spirit to work in our lives, and as we grow in our relationship with Him, we should become more and more like God.

This will affect both our thoughts and our actions. For Christians, love is a verb, and as we grow in our understanding of God's love we will start to look like Him more and more-both in who we are and what we do.

SHARE YOUR STORY

EACH OF US HAS A STORY. THE EVENTS OF OUR LIFE—GOOD, BAD, WONDERFUL OR CHALLENGING—HAVE SHAPED WHO WE ARE. GOD KNOWS YOUR STORY, AND HE INTENDS TO REDEEM IT—TO USE EVERY STRUGGLE AND EVERY JOY TO ULTIMATELY BRING YOU TO HIMSELF. WHEN WE SHARE OUR STORIES WITH OTHERS, WE GIVE THEM THE OPPORTUNITY TO SEE GOD AT WORK.

WHEN WE SHARE OUR STORIES, WE ALSO REALIZE WE ARE NOT ALONE—THAT WE HAVE COMMON EXPERIENCES AND THOUGHTS, AND THAT OTHERS CAN UNDERSTAND WHAT WE ARE GOING THROUGH. YOUR STORY CAN ENCOURAGE SOMEONE ELSE. AND TELLING IT CAN LEAD TO A PATH OF FREEDOM FOR YOU AND FOR THOSE YOU SHARE IT WITH.

1. Open your group with prayer. This should be a brief, simple prayer, in which you invite God to give you insight as you study. You can pray for specific requests at the end of the meeting, or stop momentarily to pray if a particular situation comes up during your discussion.

2. Before you start this first meeting, get contact information for every participant. Take time to pass around a copy of the Life Group Roster on page 109, a sheet of paper, or one of you pass your Study Guide, opened to the Life Group Roster. Ask someone to make copies or type up a list with everyone's information and email it to the group during the week.

3. Then, begin your time together by using the following questions and activities to get people talking.

   • What brought you here? What do you hope to get out of this group?

   • What does generosity mean to you?

   • How do you see God as generous? In what ways is He generous with you?

4. Whether your group is new or ongoing, it's always important to reflect on and review your values together. On page 104 is a Life Group Agreement with the values we've found most useful in sustaining healthy, balanced groups. We recommend that you choose one or two values—ones you haven't previously focused on or have room to grow in—to emphasize during this study. Choose ones that will take your group to the next stage of intimacy and spiritual health.

- We recommend you rotate host homes on a regular basis and let the hosts lead the meeting. Studies show that healthy groups rotate leadership. This helps to develop every member's ability to shepherd a few people in a safe environment. Even Jesus gave others the opportunity to serve alongside Him (Mark 6:30-44). Look at the FAQs in the *Appendicies* for additional infor-mation about hosting or leading the group.

- The Life Group Calendar on page 106 is a tool for planning who will host and lead each meeting. Take a few minutes to plan hosts and leaders for your remaining meetings. Don't skip this import-ant step! It will revolutionize your group.

> IF YOUR GROUP IS NEW, WELCOME NEWCOMERS. INTRODUCE EVERYONE—YOU MAY EVEN WANT TO HAVE NAME TAGS FOR YOUR FIRST MEETING.

WATCH
THE DVD

Use this space for notes to record key thoughts, questions and things you want to remember or follow up on. After watching the video, have someone read the discussion questions in the *Hear God's Story* section and direct the discussion among the group. As you go through each of the subsequent sections, ask someone else to read the questions and direct the discussion.

HEAR GOD'S STORY

THIS WEEK WE'RE TALKING ABOUT OUR IDENTITY; AS PEOPLE MADE IN GOD'S IMAGE, WE REFLECT HIS CHARACTER IN MANY WAYS, INCLUDING OUR GENEROSITY. WHEN WE ALLOW THE HOLY SPIRIT TO WORK IN OUR LIVES, WE BECOME MORE LIKE GOD AND HE EMPOWERS US TO BE GENEROUS THE WAY HE IS GENEROUS. AS WE DIVE INTO THIS WEEK'S SCRIPTURE PASSAGE, CONSIDER HOW YOUR IDENTITY AS A CHRIST-FOLLOWER—AND YOUR EXPERIENCE OF GOD'S GENEROSITY IN YOUR OWN LIFE—SHOULD BE SHAPING THE WAY YOU GIVE.

READ 2 CORINTHIANS 9:6-11.

Remember this: Whoever sows sparingly will also reap sparingly, and whoever sows generously will also reap generously. Each of you should give what you have decided in your heart to give, not reluctantly or under compulsion, for God loves a cheerful giver. And God is able to bless you abundantly, so that in all things at all times, having all that you need, you will abound in every good work. As it is written:

"They have freely scattered their gifts to the poor; their righteousness endures forever."

Now he who supplies seed to the sower and bread for food will also supply and increase your store of seed and will enlarge the harvest of your righteousness. You will be enriched in every way so that you can be generous on every occasion, and through us your generosity will result in thanksgiving to God.

1. What does it mean to give cheerfully? Does that word characterize your giving, or do you give reluctantly? (Interesting note: The Greek word used for "cheerful," actually means "with hilarity!")

....
....
....
....
....
....
....

2. What is the promise in verse 8? Does that change your attitude toward giving?

....
....
....
....

3. Why does God "enrich" us? (verse 11)

....
....
....
....

4. How does generosity result in thanksgiving?

....
....
....
....

STUDY NOTES

If anyone is poor among your fellow Israelites in any of the towns of the land the LORD your God is giving you, do not be hardhearted or tightfisted toward them. Rather, be openhanded and freely lend them whatever they need. Be careful not to harbor this wicked thought: "The seventh year, the year for canceling debts, is near," so that you do not show ill will toward the needy among your fellow Israelites and give them nothing. They may then appeal to the LORD against you, and you will be found guilty of sin. Give generously to them and do so without a grudging heart; then because of this the LORD your God will bless you in all your work and in everything you put your hand to.There will always be poor people in the land. Therefore I command you to be openhanded toward your fellow Israelites who are poor and needy in your land.

Deuteronomy 15:7-11

As the Israelites prepared to move into the Promised Land, God gave them many instructions about how to live and how to treat each other. One of these instructions was a command that every seven years they were to cancel all debts they had made to each other. Every creditor was to completely forgive any open loan he had made to a fellow Israelite, and after this "Sabbath year" it would be as if the debt had never existed.

This was an amazing way God provided for His people. If the Israelites followed this plan, there would never be any generational poverty. Even if a family or group of people experienced a financial downfall, they would have the opportunity to rebuild their lives in six years or less.

In this passage, God is reminding the people that this practice is intended to bring freedom and hope, so those with money shouldn't refuse to loan it just because the debt might only last a year or two. In addition, He challenges His chosen people to be generous and not "tightfisted" with all who are in need. Note that, as in the other passages we're studying this week, this is both a heart issue (verse 10) and a hands issue (verse 11)—God is concerned not only that we love those around us, but that we show it in practical ways.

GOD CHALLENGES HIS CHOSEN PEOPLE TO BE GENEROUS AND NOT "TIGHTFISTED" WITH ALL WHO ARE IN NEED.

CREATE A NEW STORY

GOD WANTS YOU TO BE PART OF HIS KINGDOM—TO WEAVE YOUR STORY INTO HIS. THAT WILL MEAN CHANGE—TO GO HIS WAY RATHER THAN YOUR OWN. THIS WON'T HAPPEN OVERNIGHT, BUT IT SHOULD HAPPEN STEADILY. BY STARTING WITH SMALL, SIMPLE CHOICES, WE BEGIN TO CHANGE OUR DIRECTION. THE HOLY SPIRIT HELPS US ALONG THE WAY— GIVING US GIFTS TO SERVE THE BODY, OFFERING US INSIGHTS INTO SCRIPTURE, AND CHALLENGING US TO LOVE NOT ONLY THOSE AROUND US BUT THOSE FAR FROM GOD.

IN THIS SECTION, TALK ABOUT HOW YOU WILL APPLY THE WISDOM YOU'VE LEARNED FROM THE TEACHING AND BIBLE STUDY. THEN THINK ABOUT PRACTICAL STEPS YOU CAN TAKE IN THE COMING WEEK TO LIVE OUT WHAT YOU'VE LEARNED.

1. Is it possible to love someone without being generous to them?

....

....

....

2. Why does love require doing and not just saying?

....

....

....

3. Reflect on the idea that there are many costs to owning something: the financial expense, the expense of energy, and the expense of time. Have you found this to be true in your own life? How does it affect what you buy?

....

....

....

4. Take a look at the **Circles of Life** diagram below and write the names of two or three people you know who need to know Christ. Commit to praying for God's guidance and an opportunity to share with each of them. Perhaps they would be open to joining the group? Share your lists with the group so you can all be praying for the people you've identified.

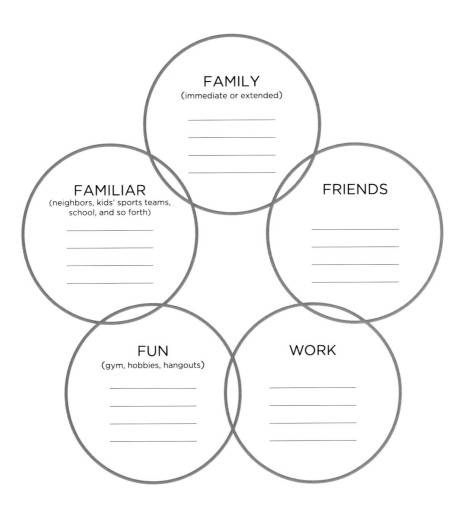

FAMILY
(immediate or extended)

FAMILIAR
(neighbors, kids' sports teams, school, and so forth)

FRIENDS

FUN
(gym, hobbies, hangouts)

WORK

5. Also consider someone—in this group or outside it—that you can begin going deeper with in an intentional way. This might be your mom or dad, a cousin, an aunt or uncle, a roommate, a college buddy, or a neighbor. Choose someone who might be open to "doing life" with you at a deeper level and pray about that opportunity.

6. This week how will you interact with the Bible? Can you commit to spending time in daily prayer or study of God's Word (use the *Daily Devotions* section to guide you)? Tell the group how you plan to follow Jesus this week, and then, at your next meeting, talk about your progress and challenges.

7. Stack your hands just a sports team does in the huddle and commit to taking a risk and going deeper in your group and in your relationships with each other.

8. To close your time together, spend some time worshipping God together—praying, singing, reading scripture.

   • Have someone use their musical gifts to lead the group in a worship song. Try singing acapella, using a worship CD, or having someone accompany your singing with a musical instrument.

   • Choose a Psalm or other favorite verse and read it aloud together. Make it a time of praise and worship, as the words remind you of all God has done for you.

   • Ask, "How can we pray for you this week?" Invite everyone to share, but don't force the issue. Be sure to write prayer requests on your Prayer and Praise Report on page 110.

   • Close your meeting with prayer.

BECAUSE OF THE SERVICE BY WHICH YOU HAVE PROVED YOURSELVES, OTHERS WILL PRAISE GOD FOR THE OBEDIENCE THAT ACCOMPANIES YOUR CONFESSION OF THE GOSPEL OF CHRIST, AND FOR YOUR GENEROSITY IN SHARING WITH THEM AND WITH EVERYONE ELSE.

2 CORINTHIANS 9:13

FOR ADDITIONAL STUDY

READ 1 TIMOTHY 6:17-19.

1. According to this passage, is it wrong to be wealthy?

   ....

   ....

   ....

2. How do we know if we are putting our hope in God or in money?

   ....

   ....

   ....

3. How can we use our earthly treasure to build up eternal treasure?

   ....

   ....

   ....

1. What should our response
   be when God gives us
   good things?

   ....
   ....
   ....
   ....
   ....
   ....
   ....

2. What sin do we tend to fall
   into when we experience
   these blessings?

   ....
   ....
   ....
   ....
   ....

3. Why is it so important to
   remember the source of
   our abilities?

   ....
   ....
   ....
   ....
   ....
   ....

DAILY DEVOTIONS

DAY 1 • READ JAMES 1:17.

Every good and perfect gift is from above, coming down from the Father of the heavenly lights, who does not change like shifting shadows.

RESPOND:

Why is it so important to recognize that everything good comes from God?

....

....

DAY 2 • READ PROVERBS 11:25.

A generous person will prosper; whoever refreshes others will be refreshed.

RESPOND:

Does it seem backwards to you that you prosper by being generous? How can you "refresh" yourself by refreshing others?

....

....

DAY 3 • READ PSALM 37:21.

The wicked borrow and do not repay, but the righteous give generously.

RESPOND:

Are there unpaid debts that are keeping you from being generous? What is one step you can take this week to eliminate those debts?

....

....

DAY 4 • READ DEUTERONOMY 16:17.

Each of you must bring a gift in proportion to the way the LORD your God has blessed you.

RESPOND:

How does God's generosity precede our generosity?

....

....

DAY 5 • READ ACTS 20:35.

"In everything I did, I showed you that by this kind of hard work we must help the weak, remembering the words the Lord Jesus himself said: 'It is more blessed to give than to receive.'"

RESPOND:

It can be difficult to work hard and then give part of our earnings to others. As we finish this week and look forward to the rest of this study, take a few minutes to ask God for His spirit to move in your life and give you wisdom as we learn together.

....

....

DAY 6

Use the following space to write any thoughts God has put in your heart and mind about the things we have looked at in this session and during your *Daily Devotions* time this week.

....

....

....

....

....

....

LOVE DOES

PURPOSEFULLY

Then Jesus came to them and said, "All authority in
heaven and on earth has been given to me. Therefore go and make disciples of all nations, baptizing
them in the name of the Father and of the Son and
of the Holy Spirit, and teaching them to obey everything I have commanded you. And surely I am with you
always, to the very end of the age."
Matthew 28:18-20

In 1966, CBS premiered the TV show Mission: Impossible. Each week, the "Impossible Missions Force" fought the forces of evil, usually after receiving instructions that self-destructed. In 1996, Paramount Pictures revived the franchise with a movie version featuring Tom Cruise. It was so successful that it led to four sequels that have made over 2 billion dollars.

When you became a Christ-follower, there was no self-destructing video message with secret instructions, but at that moment you joined a group of people with a mission. For two thousand years, that group—the church—has been working together, across the decades and around the world, to reach everyone on earth with the good news about Jesus. This is our mission, the Great Co-Mission that we partner with God to do, sharing the good news of God's Kingdom and showing love to every person. Christians are a people with a purpose—a mission that's very possible when we're walking with God.

SHARE YOUR STORY

AS WE SAID LAST WEEK, WHEN WE SHARE OUR STORIES WITH OTHERS, WE GIVE THEM THE OPPORTUNITY TO SEE GOD AT WORK. YOUR STORY IS BEING SHAPED, EVEN IN THIS MOMENT, BY BEING PART OF THIS GROUP. IN FACT, FEW THINGS CAN SHAPE US MORE THAN COMMUNITY.

WHEN WE SHARE OUR STORIES, WE CAN ENCOURAGE SOMEONE ELSE, AND LEARN. WE EXPERIENCE THE PRESENCE OF GOD AS HE HELPS US BE BRAVE ENOUGH TO REVEAL OUR THOUGHTS AND FEELINGS.

1. Open your group with prayer. This should be a brief, simple prayer in which you invite God to be with you as you meet. You can pray for specific requests at the end of the meeting, or stop momentarily to pray if a particular situation comes up during your discussion.

2. Begin your time together by using the following questions and activities to get people talking:

   • Do you have a personal mission statement for yourself or your family?

   • Briefly share a memory of someone showing compassion to you during a difficult time.

   • In the last session we asked you to write some names in the Circles of Life diagram. Who did you identify as the people in your life who need to meet Jesus? Go back to the *Circles of Life* diagram on page 25 to help you think of various people you come in contact with on a regular basis; people who need to know Jesus more deeply. Consider ideas for action and make a plan to follow through on one of them this week.

   • Pair up with someone in your group. (We suggest that men partner with men and women with women.) This person will be your spiritual partner for the rest of this study. He or she doesn't have to be your best friend. Instead, this person will simply encourage you to complete the goals you set for yourself during this study. Following through on a resolution is tough when you're on your own; it makes all the difference to have a partner to cheer you on.

WATCH
THE DVD

Use this space for notes to record key thoughts, questions and things you want to remember or follow up on. After watching the video, have someone read the discussion questions in the *Hear God's Story* section and direct the discussion among the group. As you go through each of the subsequent sections, ask someone else to read the questions and direct the discussion.

HEAR GOD'S STORY

MATTHEW CHAPTER 9 IS THE PERFECT EXAMPLE OF JESUS PRACTICING WHAT HE PREACHED AND PREACHING WHAT HE PRACTICED.

READ MATTHEW 9:1–10:8.

1. There are several examples in chapter nine of the "compassion/Kingdom" model, when Jesus shows compassion to people and then talks to them about the Kingdom of God. Identify each time Jesus uses this approach.

....

....

....

....

2. What does Jesus command His followers to do at the conclusion of this chapter?

....

....

....

....

3. In 9:37-38, Jesus tells his disciples to pray for Kingdom workers. In the beginning of chapter ten, who are the first answers to that prayer?

....

....

....

....

....

....

4. In 10:1 He calls the twelve "disciples" which means "disciplined follower." However, in verse two He calls them "apostles" which means, "one who is sent." How is this significant in light of verses 6-8?

....

....

....

....

....

....

....

....

5. With what attitude are they to do this work? (verse 8)

....

....

....

....

....

STUDY NOTES

Jesus went through all the towns and villages, teaching in their synagogues, proclaiming the good news of the kingdom and healing every disease and sickness. When he saw the crowds, he had compassion on them, because they were harassed and helpless, like sheep without a shepherd.Then he said to his disciples, "The harvest is plentiful but the workers are few. Ask the Lord of the harvest, therefore, to send out workers into his harvest field."

In the Greek, the word for "compassion" in verse 36 is "splagna," which means one's guts. The ancient Greeks knew that when we really feel empathy in our hearts we can also feel it in our bodies. In fact, sometimes we almost physically hurt in our deepest places for the needs of others. This is the kind of compassion that Jesus had for hurting people, and the compassion He calls us to have for the lost people in our world. It takes guts to share our faith and share our resources—literally!

WHEN WE REALLY FEEL EMPATHY IN OUR HEARTS WE CAN ALSO FEEL IT IN OUR BODIES.

CREATE A NEW STORY

IN THIS SECTION, TALK ABOUT HOW YOU WILL APPLY THE WISDOM YOU'VE LEARNED FROM THE TEACHING AND BIBLE STUDY. THEN THINK ABOUT PRACTICAL STEPS YOU CAN TAKE IN THE COMING WEEK TO LIVE OUT WHAT YOU'VE LEARNED.

1. Is it a new idea for you that the church is a group of people and not a building?

   ....

   ....

2. How did Jesus' acts of compassion open the door for people to hear His teaching?

   ....

   ....

3. How are you sharing your time? Your treasure? Your testimony?

   ....

   ....

4. How does giving money further the mission? What is the connection between our generosity and our participation in the mission?

   ....

   ....

5. Here are some simple ways to connect with God. Tell the group which ones you plan to try this week, and talk about your progress and challenges when you meet next time.

- Prayer. Commit to personal prayer and daily connection with God. You may find it helpful to write your prayers in a journal.

- Devotions. The *Daily Devotions* provided in each session offer an opportunity to read a short Bible passage five days a week during the course of our study. In our hurry-up world, we often move too quickly through everything—even reading God's Word! Slow down. Don't just skim, but take time to read carefully and reflect on the passage. Write down your insights on what you read each day. Copy a portion of scripture on a card and tape it somewhere in your line of sight, such as your car's dashboard or the bathroom mirror. Or text it to yourself! Think about it when you sit at red lights or while you're eating a meal. Reflect on what God is saying to you through these words. On the sixth day summarize what God has shown you throughout the week.

- To close your time together, spend some time worshipping God together—praying, singing, or reading scripture.

- Have someone use their musical gifts to lead the group in a worship song. Try singing acapella, using a worship CD, or having someone accompany your singing with a musical instrument.

- Choose a Psalm or other favorite verse and read it aloud together. Make it a time of praise and worship, as the words remind you of all God has done for you.

- Ask, "How can we pray for you this week?" Invite everyone to share, but don't force the issue. Be sure to write prayer requests on your Prayer and Praise Report on page 110.

6. Close your meeting with prayer.

FOR ADDITIONAL STUDY

READ ACTS 3.

1. How did Peter's act of compassion cause people to ask questions about Jesus?

....

....

2. What was his response to their questions?

....

....

3. You're not going to heal someone and you're not going to tell a crowd that they crucified Jesus! But there are aspects of Peter's message in verses 11–24 that can help us respond to the questions of others. What are some things we can learn from his response?

....

....

READ ACTS 4:1-22.

1. How did Peter's act of
   compassion in Chapter 3 lead
   to even more questions? Who
   is asking in this chapter, and
   how do their questions differ?

2. What can we learn from
   Peter's response in
   verses 8-12?

3. How does our church
   combine compassion with the
   Gospel message?

DAILY DEVOTIONS

DAY 1 • READ PHILIPPIANS 2:12-13.

Therefore, my dear friends, as you have always obeyed—not only in my presence, but now much more in my absence—continue to work out your salvation with fear and trembling, for it is God who works in you to will and to act in order to fulfill his good purpose.

RESPOND:

Based on our study this week, what are two main purposes for your life? How can you "work out your salvation" to fulfill those purposes?

....

....

....

DAY 2 • READ PROVERBS 19:21

Many are the plans in a person's heart, but it is the LORD's purpose that prevails.

RESPOND:

As we reflect on our purpose this week, it's important to remember that God is sovereign and ultimately He is in charge! Ask Him for wisdom in living out His mission.

....

....

....

DAY 3 • READ MATTHEW 5:14-16

You are the light of the world. A town built on a hill cannot be hidden. Neither do people light a lamp and put it under a bowl. Instead they put it on its stand, and it gives light to everyone in the house. In the same way, let your light shine before others, that they may see your good deeds and glorify your Father in heaven.

RESPOND:

Being on mission with Jesus means shining His love to everyone we meet. How can serving others and showing compassion bring glory to Him?

....

....

DAY 4 • READ 2 TIMOTHY 1:9

He has saved us and called us to a holy life—not because of anything we have done but because of his own purpose and grace.

RESPOND:

How does God's grace influence your own generosity with others? How do His purposes call you to a holy life?

....

....

DAY 5 • READ MICAH 6:8

He has shown you, O mortal, what is good. And what does the LORD require of you? To act justly and to love mercy and to walk humbly with your God.

RESPOND:

Some people memorize this verse as a summary of everything we've talked about this week: our mission in life is to love other people, show God's love, and follow Him daily. Reflect on this mission and ask God to help you grow in each area over the coming weeks.

....

....

DAY 6

Use the following space to write any thoughts God has put in your heart and mind about the things we have looked at in this session and during your *Daily Devotions* time this week.

....

....

....

....

....

....

....

....

....

....

....

....

....

....

....

LOVE DOES

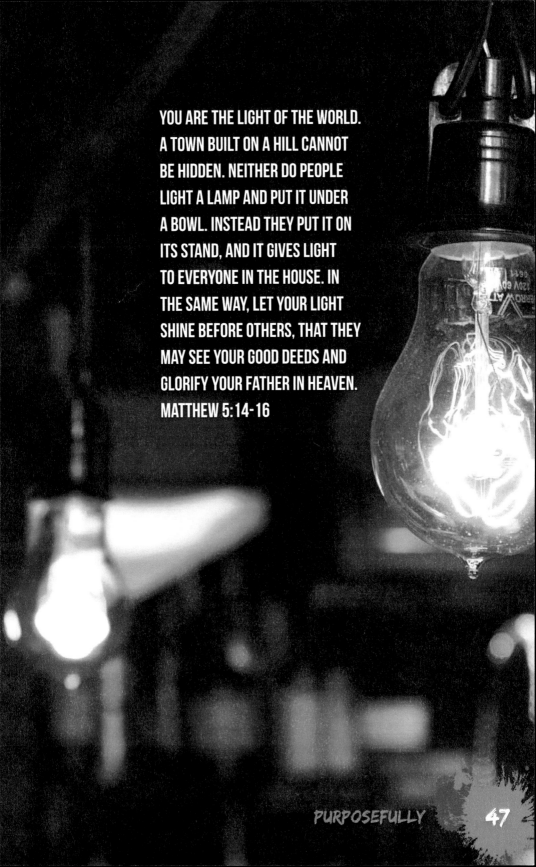

YOU ARE THE LIGHT OF THE WORLD.
A TOWN BUILT ON A HILL CANNOT
BE HIDDEN. NEITHER DO PEOPLE
LIGHT A LAMP AND PUT IT UNDER
A BOWL. INSTEAD THEY PUT IT ON
ITS STAND, AND IT GIVES LIGHT
TO EVERYONE IN THE HOUSE. IN
THE SAME WAY, LET YOUR LIGHT
SHINE BEFORE OTHERS, THAT THEY
MAY SEE YOUR GOOD DEEDS AND
GLORIFY YOUR FATHER IN HEAVEN.
MATTHEW 5:14-16

SESSION THREE

LOVE DOES

PURELY

Dear children, let us not love with words or speech
but with actions and in truth.
1 John 3:18

48 LOVE DOES

We may understand that the character of God is rooted in generosity toward us and that we are created in His image. We may understand that we are called to be part of God's mission in the world and we may even have true compassion for those who are lost. But it's still hard to be a cheerful giver!

There's a great story about a pastor in a rural area talking to one of the local farmers. The pastor asks the farmer, "If you had one hundred horses, would you give me fifty?" The farmer says, "Certainly." The pastor asks, "If you had one hundred cows, would you give me fifty?" The farmer says, "Yes, definitely." Then the pastor asks, "If you had two pigs, would you give me one?" And the farmer says, "Hey, wait a minute! You know I have two pigs!"

Generosity sounds good in the abstract, but the reality can be very difficult. Today we're going to look at several stories that show us what it means to be truly generous, and why that's part of a love that does.

SHARE YOUR STORY

OPEN YOUR GROUP WITH PRAYER. THIS SHOULD BE A BRIEF, SIMPLE PRAYER IN WHICH YOU INVITE GOD TO BE WITH YOU AS YOU MEET. YOU CAN PRAY FOR SPECIFIC REQUESTS AT THE END OF THE MEETING, OR STOP MOMENTARILY TO PRAY IF A PARTICULAR SITUATION COMES UP DURING YOUR DISCUSSION.

SHARING PERSONAL STORIES BUILDS DEEPER CONNECTIONS AMONG GROUP MEMBERS. BEGIN YOUR TIME TOGETHER BY USING THE FOLLOWING QUESTIONS AND ACTIVITIES TO GET PEOPLE TALKING.

1. Are your possessions and your money a reward from God for good behavior?

   ....

   ....

   ....

   ....

2. If we looked at your credit card bills or your checking account, what would it tell us about your priorities?

   ....

   ....

   ....

   ....

3. Sit with your spiritual partner. If your partner is absent or you are new to the group, join with another pair or someone who doesn't yet have a partner. If you haven't established your spiritual partnership yet, do it now. (See *Share Your Story* in Session Two on page 34.)

WATCH
THE DVD

Use this space for notes to record key thoughts, questions and things you want to remember or follow up on. After watching the video, have someone read the discussion questions in the *Hear God's Story* section and direct the discussion among the group. As you go through each of the subsequent sections, ask someone else to read the questions and direct the discussion.

HEAR GOD'S STORY

USE THE FOLLOWING QUESTIONS TO GUIDE YOUR DISCUSSION OF THE TEACHING AND STORIES YOU JUST EXPERIENCED ON THE DVD AND THE BIBLE PASSAGE BELOW.

READ LUKE 12:13-21.

Someone in the crowd said to him, "Teacher, tell my brother to divide the inheritance with me."

Jesus replied, "Man, who appointed me a judge or an arbiter between you?" Then he said to them, "Watch out! Be on your guard against all kinds of greed; life does not consist in an abundance of possessions."

And he told them this parable: "The ground of a certain rich man yielded an abundant harvest. He thought to himself, 'What shall I do? I have no place to store my crops.'

"Then he said, 'This is what I'll do. I will tear down my barns and build bigger ones, and there I will store my surplus grain.And I'll say to myself, "You have plenty of grain laid up for many years. Take life easy; eat, drink and be merry."'

"But God said to him, 'You fool! This very night your life will be demanded from you. Then who will get what you have prepared for yourself?'

"This is how it will be with whoever stores up things for themselves but is not rich toward God."

1. What are some of the kinds of greed Jesus might have been referring to in verse 15?

....

....

....

....

....

2. Was it wrong for the rich man to have so many crops? What is he guilty of in this parable?

....

....

....

....

....

3. Does considering your mortality change the way you look at your possessions?

....

....

....

....

....

4. What does it mean to be "rich toward God"?

....

....

....

....

....

....

STUDY NOTES

IN A BLOG POST ON THE WEBSITE PATHEOS.COM, DAVID HENSON REFLECTS ON THE STORY OF THE RICH YOUNG RULER AND OFFERS AN ALTERNATE VIEW OF THE YOUNG MAN'S RESPONSE TO JESUS.

HE WRITES:

"We have been taught the rich man goes away sad because he refuses to sell his possessions and let go of his wealth. He loves money more than he loves God. Because he cannot serve both God and mammon, the rich man chooses mammon and leaves, rejecting Jesus' command to sell his fortune….. This narrow interpretation reveals not just a lack of imagination on our part. It reveals, more importantly, our own bias for the wealthy, as the world's wealthiest. Because of our own wealth and love of money, we cannot fathom an ending other than one in which the rich man remains rich. We cannot imagine a rich man would willingly sell his possessions to follow Jesus. We cannot do so precisely because we hold so tightly to our own possessions and wealth. We cannot imagine selling our own stuff and giving the money to the poor, so surely this must be the case with the rich man in the story.

"We can only imagine how sad we would be if we really thought Jesus meant what he said to the rich man. We can only imagine how much we would grieve if we had to choose between God and mammon. Because we know which we would choose, and it isn't God. We know that because we choose it every day.

"But what if the opposite is true in this story? What if the rich man goes away sad precisely because he has chosen God over mammon? What if he is sad because he is going away to sell all his possessions and give the money to the poor in order to follow Jesus? What if he is dejected because he finally knows the cost of following God and he intends to do it?

"n this interpretation of the story, the rich man is sad not because Jesus' expectations are so high that no reasonable person (like us!) would try to meet them, but because he intends to meet them and knows how difficult it will be. What do you think? How does your identification with the Rich Young Ruler affect your reading of the story?"

CREATE A NEW STORY

IN THIS SECTION, TALK ABOUT HOW YOU WILL APPLY THE WISDOM YOU'VE LEARNED FROM THE TEACHING AND BIBLE STUDY. THEN THINK ABOUT P GOD WANTS YOU TO BE PART OF HIS KINGDOM—TO WEAVE YOUR STORY INTO HIS. THAT WILL MEAN CHANGE. IT WILL REQUIRE YOU TO GO HIS WAY RATHER THAN YOUR OWN. THIS WON'T HAPPEN OVERNIGHT, BUT IT SHOULD HAPPEN STEADILY. BY MAKING SMALL, SIMPLE CHOICES, WE CAN BEGIN TO CHANGE OUR DIRECTION. THE HOLY SPIRIT HELPS US ALONG THE WAY, BY GIVING US GIFTS TO SERVE THE BODY, OFFERING US INSIGHTS INTO SCRIPTURE, AND CHALLENGING US TO LOVE NOT ONLY THOSE AROUND US BUT THOSE FAR FROM GOD.

IN THIS SECTION, TALK ABOUT HOW YOU WILL APPLY THE WISDOM YOU'VE LEARNED IN THIS SESSION, AND THE PRACTICAL STEPS YOU CAN TAKE IN THE COMING WEEK TO LIVE OUT WHAT YOU'VE LEARNED.

1. Why is following Jesus about much more than following rules? How does pure generosity differ from rule following?

....

....

2. How does wealth make it more difficult to follow God?

....

....

3. How do you react to the idea that if you are American, you are rich by the world's standards? If God considers you "rich," how does that affect your understanding of today's teaching?

....

....

4. If God's generosity extends to the entire world, what does that mean for our generosity?

....

....

5. What steps will you take this week to grow in your relationship with God? If you've focused on prayer in past weeks, maybe you'll want to direct your attention to scripture this week. If you've been reading God's Word consistently, perhaps you'll want to take it deeper and try memorizing a verse. Tell the group which one you plan to try this week, and talk about your progress and challenges when you meet next time.

....

....

6. To close this session, spend some time worshipping God together— praying, singing, or reading scripture.

   • Have someone use their musical gifts to lead the group in a worship song. Try singing acapella, using a worship CD, or having someone accompany your singing with a musical instrument.

   • Choose a Psalm or other favorite verse and read it aloud together. Make it a time of praise and worship, as the words remind you of all God has done for you.

   • Ask, "How can we pray for you this week?" Invite everyone to share, but don't force the issue. Be sure to write prayer requests on your Prayer and Praise Report on page 110.

7. Close your meeting with prayer.

FOR ADDITIONAL STUDY

READ LUKE 19:1-10.

1. In the ancient Middle East, it was considered extremely undignified for a man to run. What does this tell you about Zacchaeus' desire to see Jesus?

    ....

    ....

2. Why do you think Jesus began the conversation by inviting himself to Zacchaeus' house?

    ....

    ....

3. Why did it bother the people so much that Jesus wanted to spend time with Zacchaeus?

    ....

    ....

4. How did Zacchaeus demonstrate that love is something you do?

    ....

    ....

READ 2 CORINTHIANS 8:1-7 AND 9:1-5.

1. How can poverty actually lead to generosity?

....
....
....
....
....
....

2. How is the ability to give a grace from God? (8:1, 6)? How is it a privilege? (8:4)

....
....
....
....
....

3. What is a way our generosity can influence other believers? (9:2)

....
....
....
....
....
....

DAILY DEVOTIONS

DAY 1 • READ 1 CORINTHIANS 15:58

Therefore, my dear brothers and sisters, stand firm. Let nothing move you. Always give yourselves fully to the work of the Lord, because you know that your labor in the Lord is not in vain.

RESPOND:

Ask God for insight into how you can give yourself fully to the Lord's work—and the help of the Holy Spirit to take action on what He reveals to you!

....

....

....

DAY 2 • READ ISAIAH 55:2

Why spend money on what is not bread, and your labor on what does not satisfy? Listen, listen to me, and eat what is good, and you will delight in the richest of fare.

RESPOND:

There's nothing wrong with having possessions, but ultimately they will not satisfy our hearts. How does this verse teach us to get what really matters?

....

....

....

LOVE DOES

DAY 3 • READ PROVERBS 21:21

Whoever pursues righteousness and love finds life, prosperity and honor.

RESPOND:

When we pursue the things of God, He promises to bless us. How can you pursue more righteousness in your life?

....

....

....

DAY 4 • READ PSALM 23:1

The LORD is my shepherd, I lack nothing.

RESPOND:

How does the Lord "shepherd" you? Thank Him for the way He provides for you each day.

....

....

....

DAY 5 • READ PROVERBS 11:24

One person gives freely, yet gains even more; another withholds unduly, but comes to poverty.

RESPOND:

What principle of giving in God's kingdom does this verse teach? Why do we so often "withhold unduly"?

....

....

....

....

DAY 6

Use the following space to write any thoughts God has put in your heart and mind about the things we have looked at in this session and during your *Daily Devotions* time this week.

....

....

....

....

....

....

....

....

....

....

....

....

....

....

WHY SPEND MONEY ON WHAT IS NOT BREAD, AND YOUR LABOR ON WHAT DOES NOT SATISFY? LISTEN, LISTEN TO ME, AND EAT WHAT IS GOOD, AND YOU WILL DELIGHT IN THE RICHEST OF FARE.

ISAIAH 55:2

SESSION FOUR

LOVE DOES
EXPECTANTLY

In everything I did, I showed you that by this kind of
hard work we must help the weak, remembering the
words the Lord Jesus himself said: 'It is more blessed
to give than to receive.'
Acts 20:35

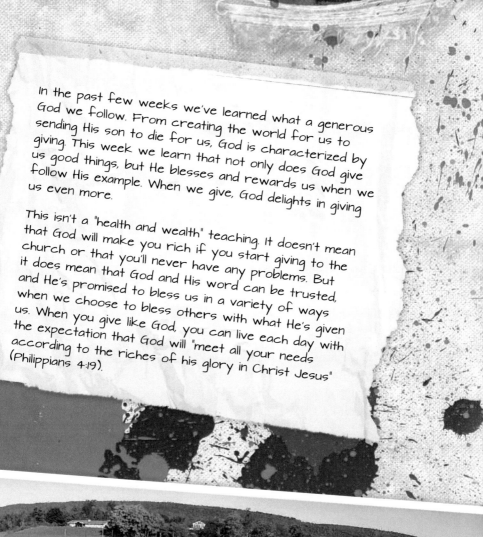

In the past few weeks we've learned what a generous God we follow. From creating the world for us to sending His son to die for us, God is characterized by giving. This week we learn that not only does God give us good things, but He blesses and rewards us when we follow His example. When we give, God delights in giving us even more.

This isn't a "health and wealth" teaching. It doesn't mean that God will make you rich if you start giving to the church or that you'll never have any problems. But it does mean that God and His word can be trusted, and He's promised to bless us in a variety of ways when we choose to bless others with what He's given us. When you give like God, you can live each day with the expectation that God will "meet all your needs according to the riches of his glory in Christ Jesus" (Philippians 4:19).

EXPECTANTLY

SHARE YOUR STORY

OPEN YOUR GROUP WITH PRAYER. THIS SHOULD BE A BRIEF, SIMPLE PRAYER IN WHICH YOU INVITE GOD TO BE WITH YOU AS YOU MEET. YOU CAN PRAY FOR SPECIFIC REQUESTS AT THE END OF THE MEETING OR STOP MOMENTARILY TO PRAY IF A PARTICULAR SITUATION COMES UP DURING YOUR DISCUSSION.

AS WE HAVE SAID IN PREVIOUS LESSONS, SHARING OUR PERSONAL STORIES BUILDS DEEPER CONNECTIONS AMONG GROUP MEMBERS. YOUR STORY MAY BE EXACTLY WHAT ANOTHER PERSON NEEDS TO HEAR TO ENCOURAGE OR STRENGTHEN THEM. AND YOUR LISTENING TO OTHERS' STORIES IS AN ACT OF LOVE AND KINDNESS TO THEM—AND COULD VERY WELL HELP THEM TO GROW SPIRITUALLY. BEGIN YOUR TIME TOGETHER BY USING THE FOLLOWING QUESTIONS AND ACTIVITIES TO GET PEOPLE TALKING.

1. The Bible teaches that "you reap what you sow." Have you found that to be true in your own life?

2. What is something you enjoy about giving to the church? What is difficult about giving?

3. Sit with your spiritual partner. If your partner is absent or if you are new to the group, join with another pair or someone who doesn't yet have a partner. If you haven't established your spiritual partnership yet, do it now. Share one prayer request and one thing you want to thank God for. Spend some time praying about what you've shared. (See *Share Your Story* in Session Two on page 34.)

WATCH THE DVD

Use this space for notes to record key thoughts, questions and things you want to remember or follow up on. After watching the video, have someone read the discussion questions in the *Hear God's Story* section and direct the discussion among the group. As you go through each of the subsequent sections, ask someone else to read the questions and direct the discussion.

HEAR GOD'S STORY

USE THE FOLLOWING QUESTIONS TO GUIDE YOUR DISCUSSION OF THE TEACHING FROM THE VIDEO AND THE BIBLE PASSAGE BELOW.

READ 2 CORINTHIANS 9:6-11.

Remember this: Whoever sows sparingly will also reap sparingly, and whoever sows generously will also reap generously. Each of you should give what you have decided in your heart to give, not reluctantly or under compulsion, for God loves a cheerful giver. And God is able to bless you abundantly, so that in all things at all times, having all that you need, you will abound in every good work. As it is written:

"They have freely scattered their gifts to the poor; their righteousness endures forever."

Now he who supplies seed to the sower and bread for food will also supply and increase your store of seed and will enlarge the harvest of your righteousness. You will be enriched in every way so that you can be generous on every occasion, and through us your generosity will result in thanksgiving to God.

1. What would happen if the farmer wanted to hold on to his seed and keep it instead of planting it?

....
....
....
....
....

2. How does God promise to bless us when we give cheerfully? (verse 8)

....
....
....

3. Where does our ability to sow come from? (verse 10)

....
....
....

4. What is a "harvest of righteousness"?

....
....
....

5. Why are we enriched? (verse 11)

....
....
....
....

STUDY NOTES

IN HIS BOOK TAKE GOD AT HIS WORD: EXPERIENCE THE POWER OF GIVING, DR. KREGG HOOD COMPARES OLD TESTAMENT LAW WITH NEW TESTAMENT TEACHING. FOR EXAMPLE:

OLD TESTAMENT	NEW TESTAMENT
Do not murder (Ex 20:13)	Anyone who hates his brother is a murderer.(1 John 3:15)
Do not commit adultery (Ex 20:14)	Anyone who lusts commits adultery in his heart. (Mt 5:28)
Do not swear falsely by God's name. (Lev 19:12)	Do not swear at all. (Mt 5:34)
The entire tithe will be holy to the Lord (Lev 27:32)	Give as you are prospered (1 Cor 16:2)

LOVE DOES

We have received complete forgiveness of sins, eternal life, the Holy Spirit of God, and every spiritual blessing possible through Christ. Everything in Christ is a higher standard than the Old Testament. We would be hard pressed to consider "New Testament" giving to be less than what God expected in the Old Testament.

CREATE A NEW STORY

IN THIS SECTION, TALK ABOUT HOW YOU WILL APPLY THE WISDOM YOU'VE LEARNED FROM THE TEACHING AND BIBLE STUDY. THEN THINK ABOUT PRACTICAL STEPS YOU CAN TAKE IN THE COMING WEEK TO LIVE OUT WHAT YOU'VE LEARNED.

1. What does it mean to build riches in heaven?

....

....

....

2. Sometimes Christians say, "Generosity isn't about equal giving, but equal sacrifice." What does this mean? How does the story of the widow giving at the temple illustrate this idea?

....

....

....

3. Why is it so important to remember that not only our money but also our abilities and strength come from God?

....

....

....

4. Do you have a story like Don's of God's faithfulness? Has God ever surprised you with blessings after you have given sacrificially?

....

....

....

....

5. Spend some time praying about those you know who might respond to a simple invitation: to come to a church service, to join your small group, or even just to have coffee and talk about spiritual matters. Ask the Holy Spirit to bring to mind people you can pray for.

FOR ADDITIONAL STUDY

READ MATTHEW 25:14-30.

1. One author describes the story as a process of gracious receiving and gracious giving: three servants received and accepted; two servants grew the money through investing; the first two brought all of it back plus extra; God gave them more to invest. How do both the workers and the master demonstrate gracious giving in this parable? How do they show gracious receiving?

   ....

   ....

2. Why did the third servant bury the money instead of investing it?

   ....

   ....

3. What is one insight you gain from this parable that you can apply to your life?

   ....

   ....

   ....

READ MALACHI 3:8-10 AND LEVITICUS 27:30-32.

1. What does it mean to "rob" God?

2. React to the idea in Malachi of testing God in tithing.

3. Why was the tithe called "holy to the Lord?"

DAILY DEVOTIONS

DAY 1 • READ MATTHEW 6:19-21

"Do not store up for yourselves treasures on earth, where moths and vermin destroy, and where thieves break in and steal.But store up for yourselves treasures in heaven, where moths and vermin do not destroy, and where thieves do not break in and steal. For where your treasure is, there your heart will be also.

RESPOND:

It's not wrong to own things, but our hope and our heart should not be in our possessions. Where is your treasure? Are you storing it up or stewarding it?

....

....

DAY 2 • READ HEBREWS 11:6

And without faith it is impossible to please God, because anyone who comes to him must believe that he exists and that he rewards those who earnestly seek him.

RESPOND:

Remember that God's blessings extend far beyond the financial. Ask God to increase your faith so that you might seek Him.

....

....

DAY 3 • READ PROVERBS 3:9-10

Honor the LORD with your wealth, with the firstfruits of all your crops; then your barns will be filled to overflowing, and your vats will brim over with new wine.

RESPOND:

In ancient times, wealth was measured in the literal harvest of crops instead of in money. Would it be easier or more difficult to give a tenth of your crops and cattle? How did this command teach people to trust God?

....

....

DAY 4 • READ MATTHEW 13:23

But the seed falling on good soil refers to someone who hears the word and understands it. This is the one who produces a crop, yielding a hundred, sixty or thirty times what was sown.

RESPOND:

Reaping good things in our lives begins with hearing God's word and then putting it into practice. What is one way you can sow something good for God this week?

....

....

DAY 5 • READ PROVERBS 28:27

Those who give to the poor will lack nothing, but those who close their eyes to them receive many curses.

RESPOND:

Ask God to open your eyes to the poor and needy around you, and to respond as He wants you to.

....

....

....

DAY 6

Use the following space to write any thoughts God has put in your heart and mind about the things we have looked at in this session and during your *Daily Devotions* time this week.

BUT THE SEED FALLING ON GOOD SOIL REFERS TO SOMEONE WHO HEARS THE WORD AND UNDERSTANDS IT. THIS IS THE ONE WHO PRODUCES A CROP, YIELDING A HUNDRED, SIXTY OR THIRTY TIMES WHAT WAS SOWN. MATTHEW 13:23

EXPECTANTLY

LOVE DOES
TOGETHER

Two are better than one, because they have a good
return for their labor.
Ecclesiastes 4:9

It was Nome, Alaska, in January of 1926, and six-year-old Richard Stanley showed symptoms of diphtheria. This meant there could be a huge outbreak of this very contagious disease, and when the boy passed away soon after, the local doctor began immunizing as many people as possible with an experimental but effective anti-diphtheria serum. However, the doctor did not have enough doses for the entire town, and it wasn't long before the supply ran out.

The nearest supply of more serum was in Nenana, Alaska—1000 miles of frozen wilderness away. Amazingly, a group of trappers and prospectors volunteered to cover the distance with their dog teams! Operating in relays from trading post to trapping station and beyond, the team carried the serum. Oblivious to frostbite, fatigue, and exhaustion, the teamsters mushed relentlessly until, after 144 hours in minus 50-degree winds, the serum was delivered to Nome. As a result, only one other person died, and the potentially disastrous epidemic was averted. The sacrifice of a few people gave an entire community the gift of life.

When we are willing to sacrifice and work together, amazing things can happen. As we finish this study, let's focus on what God has to say about the "teamwork" He wants from us—and how our sacrifice can bring life to our community.

SHARE YOUR STORY

OPEN YOUR GROUP WITH PRAYER. THIS SHOULD BE A BRIEF, SIMPLE PRAYER IN WHICH YOU INVITE GOD TO BE WITH YOU AS YOU MEET. YOU CAN PRAY FOR SPECIFIC REQUESTS AT THE END OF THE MEETING OR STOP MOMENTARILY TO PRAY IF A PARTICULAR SITUATION COMES UP DURING YOUR DISCUSSION.

AS WE HAVE SAID IN PREVIOUS LESSONS, SHARING OUR PERSONAL STORIES BUILDS DEEPER CONNECTIONS AMONG GROUP MEMBERS. YOUR STORY MAY BE EXACTLY WHAT ANOTHER PERSON NEEDS TO HEAR TO ENCOURAGE OR STRENGTHEN THEM. AND YOUR LISTENING TO OTHERS' STORIES IS AN ACT OF LOVE AND KINDNESS TO THEM—AND COULD VERY WELL HELP THEM TO GROW SPIRITUALLY. BEGIN YOUR TIME TOGETHER BY USING THE FOLLOWING QUESTIONS AND ACTIVITIES TO GET PEOPLE TALKING.

1. What has surprised you most about this group? Where did God meet you over the last five weeks?

. . . .

. . . .

. . . .

2. Have you ever been part of team that worked really well together? What made that team successful?

. . . .

. . . .

. . . .

3. If you won a million dollars, what would you do first? (Be honest!)

    ....

    ....

    ....

4. Take time in this final session to connect with your spiritual partner. What has God been showing you through these sessions? What positive changes has your partner noticed in you? Check in with each other about the progress you have made in your spiritual growth during this study. Make plans about whether you will continue your relationship after the group has concluded.

    ....

    ....

    ....

    ....

    ....

    ....

    ....

    ....

    ....

5. Take some time for each person to share about how they've done with inviting the people on the Circles of Life to church or your small group. What specific conversations are you praying about for the weeks to come?

    ....

    ....

    ....

    ....

    ....

    ....

    ....

WATCH
THE DVD

WATCH ONLY THE FIRST PART OF THE VIDEO AT THIS TIME. YOU'LL WATCH THE REST LATER ON IN THE *CREATE A NEW STORY* SECTION.

Use this space for notes to record key thoughts, questions and things you want to remember or follow up on. After watching the video, have someone read the discussion questions in the *Hear God's Story* section and direct the discussion among the group. As you go through each of the subsequent sections, ask someone else to read the questions and direct the discussion.

TOGETHER 85

HEAR GOD'S STORY

READ 1 CHRONICLES 29: 1-20.

1. In verse 5, David asks the people, "Now, who is willing to consecrate themselves to the Lord today?" To consecrate means to make something sacred or holy. How does this verse connect consecration to generosity?

   ....

   ....

   ....

   ....

2. How does David's example as a leader influence the response of the people?

   ....

   ....

   ....

   ....

REREAD 2 CORINTHIANS 9:7. HOW DOES THE PEOPLES' RESPONSE IN VERSE 9 ILLUSTRATE THIS PRINCIPLE?

1. Where does our generosity ultimately come from? (verses 12-14)

2. What does David's speech teach us about the importance of our attitude when giving to God?

STUDY NOTES

IN THIS WEEK'S TEACHING, DON/MIKE MENTIONS THIS PASSAGE IN 1 CORINTHIANS 16:

Now about the collection for the Lord's people: Do what I told the Galatian churches to do. On the first day of every week, each one of you should set aside a sum of money in keeping with your income, saving it up, so that when I come no collections will have to be made. Then, when I arrive, I will give letters of introduction to the men you approve and send them with your gift to Jerusalem. If it seems advisable for me to go also, they will accompany me.

He notes that Paul is teaching that Christians were to give consistently and proportionately. But who was this money going to, and why was it needed?

Both here and in other letters (such as Romans 15:26), Paul asks the believers to provide financial support for the Christians back in Jerusalem. Some scholars think this was because there was a famine in Jerusalem at the time (see Acts 11:27-30) and others think it might be because the church was giving much of its money away to support widows and others in need (Acts 6:1-6). Regardless, it's interesting that Paul is very straightforward in discussing this matter with the church while at the same time wanting to avoid any manipulation of the people based on his position—note that in verse two he says that if the people give regularly he will not need to take a special collection during his visit to them.

Today it's not common to see one church taking an offering for the support of another church, but the principles here still apply to us in our giving: we should set aside part of our money (in other words, it should be a choice we've prayed about and prepared ahead of time), "each one" of us is responsible for following God this way, and our leaders are responsible for teaching us about what it means to be generous.

CREATE A NEW STORY

IN THIS SECTION, TALK ABOUT HOW YOU WILL APPLY THE WISDOM YOU'VE LEARNED FROM THE TEACHING AND BIBLE STUDY. THEN THINK ABOUT PRACTICAL STEPS YOU CAN TAKE IN THE COMING WEEK TO LIVE OUT WHAT YOU'VE LEARNED.

1. The seven principles we studied this week were: start recognizing who owns it all; start giving now; start giving to God first; start giving to God regularly; start giving proportionately; start giving to your church first; start enjoying the generosity of God. Which principle stands out the most to you? Why?

....

....

....

....

2. Think back to lesson two, when we learned that Jesus' purpose was to build His church and that His church has a mission. Why is it so important to give to the church?

....

....

....

....

3. How do we show God's power when we work together? One of the great accomplishments God performed through our congregation in 2015 was the start of a new church in Santa Cruz, Bolivia. In one year over $90,000 was raised to build a new church building/children's center, and another $81,000 was committed to support 178 children that will attend that church. God does amazing things when His people work together generously. All of these funds were given over and above our regular giving and tithes. It is even greater to know that a major portion of our regular giving year in and year out goes to support missions in our own community, our nation, and the world. We give well over that amount every year though our weekly offerings. This is a pretty clear picture of the same thing that happened in the nation of Israel under King David's reign. Love Does Together is a powerful thing!

....

....

....

....

4. In light of the stories about church that were shared in this week's session, take a few minutes to share how CACC has affected your life or the life of someone you know.

....

....

....

....

....

5. Why is it so important to give "above and beyond" through our church family in certain seasons?

....

....

....

....

....

....

....

6. When we build, who are we building for? When we start new campuses, who are we starting those campuses for?

....

....

....

....

....

....

....

WATCH
THE DVD

WATCH THE REMAINDER OF THE VIDEO WITH A MESSAGE FROM PASTORS DON AND MIKE.

1. As this is the last meeting in this study, take some time to celebrate the work God has done in the lives of group members. Have each person in the group share some step of growth they have noticed in another member. (In other words, no one will talk about themselves. Instead, affirm others in the group.) Make sure each person gets affirmed and noticed and celebrated— whether the steps they've made are large or small.

2. If your group still needs to make decisions about continuing to meet after this session, have that discussion now. Talk about what you will study, who will lead, and where and when you will meet.

3. Review your Life Group Agreement on page 104 and evaluate how well you met your goals. Discuss any changes you want to make as you move forward. If you plan to continue meeting, and your group starts a new study, this is a great time to take on a new role or change roles of service in your group. What new role will you take on? If you are uncertain, maybe your group members have some ideas for you. Remember you aren't making a lifetime commitment to the new role; it will only be for a few weeks. Maybe someone would like to share the role with you if you don't feel ready to serve solo.

4. Close by praying for your prayer requests and take a couple of minutes to review the praises you have recorded over the past five weeks on the Prayer and Praise Report on page 110. Spend some time just worshipping God and thanking Him for all He's done in your group during this study.

FOR ADDITIONAL STUDY

EXPLORE THE BIBLE PASSAGES RELATED TO THIS SESSION'S THEME ON YOUR OWN, JOTTING YOUR REFLECTIONS IN A JOURNAL OR IN THIS STUDY GUIDE. YOU MAY EVEN WANT TO USE A BIBLE WEBSITE OR APP TO LOOK UP COMMENTARY ON THESE PASSAGES.

READ MATTHEW 6:1-4.

1. Why is it so important that we not give to impress others?

   ....

   ....

2. What does it mean to "not let your left hand know what your right is doing"? What is a real-life way to put that into practice?

   ....

   ....

   ....

   ....

3. What does God promise to do if we give in this way?

   ....

   ....

READ MATTHEW 25: 34-40.

1. What does this passage teach us about how to serve Christ?

2. What is the reward we are promised for serving this way?

3. How does serving "the least of these" point to our King?

DAILY DEVOTIONS

DAY 1 • READ MARK 8:35-36

For whoever wants to save their life will lose it, but whoever loses their life for me and for the gospel will save it. What good is it for someone to gain the whole world, yet forfeit their soul?

RESPOND:

What does it mean to lose your life for Christ?

....

....

....

....

DAY 2 • READ PROVERBS 27:17

As iron sharpens iron, so one person sharpens another.

RESPOND:

When we serve, give, and learn together, we "sharpen" each other to be more than we could be alone. How has this group sharpened you and helped you grow?

....

....

....

....

DAY 3 • READ HEBREWS 10: 24-25

And let us consider how we may spur one another on toward love and good deeds, not giving up meeting together, as some are in the habit of doing, but encouraging one another—and all the more as you see the Day approaching.

RESPOND:

How can you spur others on toward more love, more generosity, more obedience to God? How have others spurred you on in these areas?

....

....

DAY 4 • READ EPHESIANS 4:16

From him the whole body, joined and held together by every supporting ligament, grows and builds itself up in love, as each part does its work.

RESPOND:

Together we are the body of Christ, doing His work on earth. The church is only effective when every part "does its work." How can your efforts and your sacrifices help the body grow in love?

....

....

DAY 5 • READ ROMANS 15: 5-6

May the God who gives endurance and encouragement give you the same attitude of mind toward each other that Christ Jesus had, so that with one mind and one voice you may glorify the God and Father of our Lord Jesus Christ.

RESPOND:

As we finish this study, take some time to pray that God would help us to have attitudes of endurance and encouragement, and that our unity in this mission would glorify God.

....

....

....

TOGETHER

DAY 6

Use the following space to write any thoughts God has put in your heart and mind about the things we have looked at in this session and during your *Daily Devotions* time this week.

....

....

....

....

....

....

....

....

....

....

....

....

....

....

....

....

LOVE DOES

AS IRON SHARPENS
IRON, SO ONE PERSON
SHARPENS ANOTHER.
PROVERBS 27:17

TOGETHER

APPENDICES

GREAT RESOURCES TO HELP MAKE YOUR
SMALL GROUP EXPERIENCE EVEN BETTER!

FREQUENTLY ASKED QUESTIONS

WHAT DO WE DO ON THE FIRST NIGHT OF OUR GROUP?

Like all fun things in life—have a party! A "get to know you" coffee, dinner, or dessert is a great way to launch a new study. You may want to review the Life Group Agreement (pages 104–105) and share the names of a few friends you can invite to join you. But most importantly, have fun before your study time begins.

WHERE DO WE FIND NEW MEMBERS FOR OUR GROUP?

This can be troubling, especially for new groups that have only a few people or for existing groups that lose a few people along the way. We encourage you to pray with your group and then brainstorm a list of people from work, church, your neighborhood, your children's school, family, the gym, and so forth. Then have each group member invite several of the people on his or her list. Another good strategy is to ask church leaders to make an announcement or allow a bulletin insert.

No matter how you find members, it's vital that you stay on the lookout for new people to join your group. All groups tend to go through healthy attrition—the result of moves, releasing new leaders, ministry opportunities, and so forth—and if the group gets too small, it could be at risk of shutting down. If you and your group stay open, you'll be amazed at the people God sends your way. The next person just might become a friend for life. You never know!

HOW LONG WILL THIS GROUP MEET?

Most groups meet weekly for at least their first 5 weeks, but every other week can work as well. We strongly recommend that the group meet for the first six months on a weekly basis if at all possible. This allows for continuity, and if people miss a meeting they aren't gone for a whole month.

At the end of this study, each group member may decide if he or she wants to continue on for another study. Some groups launch relationships for years to come, and others are stepping-stones into another group experience. Either way, enjoy the journey.

CAN WE DO THIS STUDY ON OUR OWN?

Absolutely! This may sound crazy, but one of the best ways to do this study is not with a full house but with a few friends. You may choose to gather with another couple who would enjoy some relational time (perhaps going to the movies or having a quiet dinner) and then walking through this study. Jesus will be with you even if there are only two of you (Matthew 18:20).

WHAT IF THIS GROUP IS NOT WORKING FOR US?

You're not alone! This could be the result of a personality conflict, life stage difference, geographical distance, level of spiritual maturity, or any number of things. Relax. Pray for God's direction, and at the end of this 5-week study, decide whether to continue with this group or find another. You don't typically buy the first car you look at or marry the first person you date, and the same goes with a group. However, don't bail out before the 5 weeks are up—God might have something to teach you. Also, don't run from conflict or prejudge people before you have given them a chance. God is still working in your life, too!

WHO IS THE LEADER?

Most groups have an official leader. But ideally, the group will mature and members will rotate the leadership of meetings. We have discovered that healthy groups rotate hosts/leaders and homes on a regular basis. This model ensures that all members grow, give their unique contribution, and develop their gifts. This study guide and the Holy Spirit can keep things on track even when you rotate leaders. Christ has promised to be in your midst as you gather. Ultimately, God is your leader each step of the way.

HOW DO WE HANDLE THE CHILDCARE NEEDS IN OUR GROUP?

Very carefully. Seriously, this can be a sensitive issue. We suggest that you empower the group to openly brainstorm solutions. You may try one option that works for a while and then adjust over time. Our favorite approach is for adults to meet in the living room or dining room and to share the cost of a babysitter (or two) who can watch the kids in a different part of the house. This way, parents don't have to be away from their children all evening when their children are too young to be left at home. A second option is to use one home for the kids and a second home (close by or a phone call away) for the adults. A third idea is to rotate the responsibility of providing a lesson or care for the children either in the same home or in another home nearby. This can be an incredible blessing for kids. Finally, the most common solution is to decide that you need to have a night to invest in your spiritual lives individually or as a couple and to make your own arrangements for childcare. No matter what decision the group makes, the best approach is to dialogue openly about both the problem and the solution.

LIFE GROUP AGREEMENT

OUR PURPOSE

To provide a predictable environment where participants experience authentic community and spiritual growth.

OUR VALUES

Group Attendance

To give priority to the group meeting. We will call or email if we will be late or absent. (Completing the Life Group Calendar on page 106 will minimize this issue.)

Safe Environment

To help create a safe place where people can be heard and feel loved. (Please, no quick answers, snap judgments, or simple fixes.)

Respect Differences

To be gentle and gracious to people with different spiritual maturity, personal opinions, temperaments, or "imperfections" in fellow group members. We are all works in progress.

Confidentiality

To keep anything that is shared strictly confidential and within the group, and to avoid sharing improper information about those outside the group.

Encouragement for Growth

To be not just takers but givers of life. We want to spiritually multiply our life by serving others with our God-given gifts.

Shared Ownership

To remember that every member is a minister and to ensure that each participant will share a small team role or responsibility over time.

Rotating Hosts/Leaders

To encourage different people to rotate the responsibility of facilitating each meeting. (See the Life Group Calendar on page 106.)

OUR EXPECTATIONS

Refreshments/mealtimes _____

Childcare _____

When we will meet (day of week) _____

Where we will meet (place) _____

We will begin at (time) _____ and end at _____

We will do our best to have some or all of us attend a worship service together. Our primary worship service time will be _____

Date of this agreement _____

Date we will review this agreement again _____

Who (other than the leader) will review this agreement at the end of this study _____

LIFE GROUP CALENDAR

Planning and calendaring can help ensure the greatest participation at every meeting. At the end of each meeting, review this calendar. Be sure to include a regular rotation of host homes and leaders, and do not forget birthdays, socials, church events, holidays, and mission/ministry projects.

Date	Lesson	Host Home	Dessert/Meal	Leader
January 11	1	Steve and Laura's	Joe	Bill

SPIRITUAL PARTNERS' CHECK-IN

Briefly check in each week and write down your personal plans and progress targets for the next week (or even for the next few weeks). This could be done before or after the meeting, on the phone, through an e-mail message, or even in person from time to time.

My Name:

Spiritual Partner's Name:

	Our Plan	Our Progress
Week 1		
Week 2		
Week 3		
Week 4		
Week 5		
Week 6		

MEMORY VERSE CARDS

SESSION ONE • TITUS 3:5-7
He saved us through the washing of rebirth and renewal by the Holy Spirit, whom he poured out on us generously through Jesus Christ our Savior, so that, having been justified by his grace, we might become heirs having the hope of eternal life.

SESSION TWO • MATTHEW 28:18-20
Then Jesus came to them and said, "All authority in heaven and on earth has been given to me. Therefore go and make disciples of all nations, baptizing them in the name of the Father and of the Son and of the Holy Spirit, and teaching them to obey everything I have commanded you. And surely I am with you always, to the very end of the age."

SESSION THREE • 1 JOHN 3:18
Dear children, let us not love with words or speech but with actions and in truth.

SESSION FOUR • ACTS 20:35
In everything I did, I showed you that by this kind of hard work we must help the weak, remembering the words the Lord Jesus himself said: 'It is more blessed to give than to receive.'

SESSION FIVE • ECCLESIASTES 4:9
Two are better than one, because they have a good return for their labor.

LIFE GROUP ROSTER

NAME	PHONE	EMAIL

PRAYER REQUESTS

SESSION 1

SESSION 2

SESSION 3

SESSION 4

SESSION 5

SESSION 6

LOVE DOES

PRAISE REPORTS

LIFE GROUP LEADERS

KEY RESOURCES TO HELP YOUR LEADERSHIP
EXPERIENCE BE THE BEST IT CAN BE.

HOSTING AN OPEN HOUSE

If you're starting a new group, try planning an "open house" before your first formal group meeting. Even if you have only two to four core members, it's a great way to break the ice and to consider prayerfully who else might be open to joining you over the next few weeks. You can also use this kick-off meeting to hand out study guides, spend some time getting to know each other, discuss each person's expectations for the group and briefly pray for each other.

A simple meal or good desserts always make a kick-off meeting more fun.

After people introduce themselves and share how they ended up being at the meeting (you can play a game to see who has the wildest story!), have everyone respond to a few icebreaker questions:

- What is your favorite family vacation?

- What is one thing you love about your church/our community?

- What are three things about your life growing up that most people here don't know?

Next, ask everyone to tell what he or she hopes to get out of the study. You might want to review the Life Group Agreement and talk about each person's expectations and priorities.

Finally, set an open chair (maybe two) in the center of your group and explain that it represents someone who would enjoy or benefit from this group but who isn't here yet. Ask people to pray about inviting someone to join the group over the next few weeks. Hand out postcards and have everyone write an invitation or two. Don't worry about ending up with too many people; you can always have one discussion circle in the living room and another in the dining room after you watch the lesson. Each group could then report prayer requests and progress at the end of the session.

You can skip this kick-off meeting if your time is limited, but you'll experience a huge benefit if you take the time to connect with each other in this way.

LEADING FOR THE FIRST TIME

1. Sweaty palms are a healthy sign. The Bible says God is gracious to the humble. Remember who is in control; the time to worry is when you're not worried. Those who are soft in heart (and sweaty palmed) are those whom God is sure to speak through.

2. Seek support. Ask your leader, co-leader, or close friend to pray for you and prepare with you before the session. Walking through the study will help you anticipate potentially difficult questions and discussion topics.

3. Bring your uniqueness to the study. Lean into who you are and how God wants you to uniquely lead the study.

4. Prepare. Prepare. Prepare. Go through the session several times. If you are using the DVD, listen to the teaching segment and Leadership Lifter. Consider writing in a journal or fasting for a day to prepare yourself for what God wants to do. Don't wait until the last minute to prepare.

5. Ask for feedback so you can grow. Perhaps in an email or on cards handed out at the study, have everyone write down three things you did well and one thing you could improve on. Don't get defensive. Instead, show an openness to learn and grow.

6. Prayerfully consider launching a new group. This doesn't need to happen overnight, but God's heart is for this to take place over time. Not all Christians are called to be leaders or teachers, but we are all called to be "shepherds" of a few someday.

7. Share with your group what God is doing in your heart. God is searching for those whose hearts are fully his. Share your trials and victories. We promise that people will relate.

8. Prayerfully consider whom you would like to pass the baton to next week. It's only fair. God is ready for the next member of your group to go on the faith journey you just traveled. Make it fun, and expect God to do the rest.

LEADERSHIP TRAINING 101

CONGRATULATIONS! YOU HAVE RESPONDED TO THE CALL TO HELP SHEPHERD JESUS' FLOCK. THERE ARE FEW OTHER TASKS IN THE FAMILY OF GOD THAT SURPASS THE CONTRIBUTION YOU WILL BE MAKING. AS YOU PREPARE TO LEAD, WHETHER IT IS ONE SESSION OR THE ENTIRE SERIES, HERE ARE A FEW THOUGHTS TO KEEP IN MIND. WE ENCOURAGE YOU TO READ THESE AND REVIEW THEM WITH EACH NEW DISCUSSION LEADER BEFORE HE OR SHE LEADS.

1. Remember that you are not alone. God knows everything about you, and He knew that you would be asked to lead your group. Remember that it is common for all good leaders to feel that they are not ready to lead. Moses, Solomon, Jeremiah and Timothy were all reluctant to lead. God promises, "Never will I leave you; never will I forsake you" (Hebrews 13:5). Whether you are leading for one evening, for several weeks, or for a lifetime, you will be blessed as you serve.

2. Don't try to do it alone. Pray right now for God to help you build a healthy leadership team. If you can enlist a co-leader to help you lead the group, you will find your experience to be much richer. This is your chance to involve as many people as you can in building a healthy group. All you have to do is call and ask people to help. You'll probably be surprised at the response.

3. Just be yourself. If you won't be you, who will? God wants you to use your unique gifts and temperament. Don't try to do things exactly like another leader; do them in a way that fits you! Just admit it when you don't have an answer, and apologize when you make a mistake. Your group will love you for it, and you'll sleep better at night!

4. Prepare for your meeting ahead of time. Review the session and the leader's notes, and write down your responses to each question. Pay special attention to exercises that ask group members to do something other than engage in discussion.These exercises will help your group live what the Bible teaches, not just talk about it. Be sure you understand how an exercise works, and bring any necessary supplies (such as paper and pens) to your meeting. If the exercise employs one of the items in the appendix, be sure to look over that item so you'll know how it works. Finally, review "Outline for Each Session" so you'll remember the purpose of each section in the study.

5. Pray for your group members by name. Before you begin your session, go around the room in your mind and pray for each member by name. You may want to review the prayer list at least once a week. Ask God to use your time together to touch the heart of every person uniquely. Expect God to lead you to whomever He wants you to encourage or challenge in a special way. If you listen, God will surely lead!

6. When you ask a question, be patient. Someone will eventually respond. Sometimes people need a moment or two of silence to think about the question. Keep in mind, if silence doesn't bother you, it won't bother anyone else. After someone responds, affirm the response with a simple "thanks" or "good job." Then ask, "How about somebody else?" or "Would someone who hasn't shared like to add anything?" Be sensitive to new people or reluctant members who aren't ready to say, pray or do anything. If you give them a safe setting, they will blossom over time.

7. Provide transitions between questions. When guiding the discussion, always read aloud the transitional paragraphs and the questions. Ask the group if anyone would like to read the paragraph or Bible passage. Don't call on anyone, but ask for a volunteer, and then be patient until someone begins. Be sure to thank the person who reads aloud.

8. Break up into Life groups each week or they won't stay. If your group has more than seven people, we strongly encourage you to have the group gather sometimes in discussion circles of three or four people during the *Hear God's Story* or *Create a New Story* sections of the study. With a greater opportunity to talk in a small circle, people will connect more with the study, apply more quickly what they're learning and ultimately get more out of it. A small circle also encourages a quiet person to participate and tends to minimize the effects of a more vocal or dominant member. It can also help people feel more loved in your group. When you gather again at the end of the section, you can have one person summarize the highlights from each circle. Small circles are also helpful during prayer time. People who are unaccustomed to praying aloud will feel more comfortable trying it with just two or three others. Also, prayer requests won't take as much time, so circles will have more time to actually pray. When you gather back with the whole group, you can have one person from each circle briefly update everyone on the prayer requests. People are more willing to pray in small circles if they know that the whole group will hear all the prayer requests.

9. Rotate facilitators weekly. At the end of each meeting, ask the group who should lead the following week. Let the group help select your weekly facilitator. You may be perfectly capable of leading each time, but you will help others grow in their faith and gifts if you give them opportunities to lead. You can use the Small Group Calendar to fill in the names of all meeting leaders at once if you prefer.

10. One final challenge (for new or first time leaders): Before your first opportunity to lead, look up each of the five passages listed below. Read each one as a devotional exercise to help yourself develop a shepherd's heart. Trust us on this one. If you do this, you will be more than ready for your first meeting.

    MATTHEW 9:36

    1 PETER 5:2-4

    PSALM 23

    EZEKIEL 34:11-16

    1 THESSALONIANS 2:7-11-12

NOTES

LOVE DOES